When Safety Leaves The Home

Understanding Fear, Control, Violence, and the Human Systems That Shape Families

Jyee Byrne

WHEN SAFETY LEAVES THE HOME

Understanding Fear, Control, Violence, and the Human Systems That Shape Families

Wolfpack Edition

Important Notice

This book is an educational resource.

It is designed to increase understanding of human behaviour, emotional regulation, family systems, and the factors that contribute to emotional safety, relationship functioning, and domestic and family violence prevention.

It is **not** intended to diagnose, assess, or treat any medical, psychological, psychiatric, or legal condition. It is not a substitute for professional advice, therapy, counselling, legal representation, crisis intervention, or emergency services.

If you or someone you know is experiencing domestic or family violence, or is at immediate risk of harm, contact emergency services or your local domestic and family violence support service immediately.

Evidence and Framework Statement

The Human Operating System and The Human Hologram are educational frameworks developed by Jyee Byrne through The Wolfpack Way.

These frameworks integrate concepts informed by multiple fields of research, including developmental psychology, attachment theory, trauma research, behavioural science, neuroscience, family systems, leadership, and emotional regulation.

They are intended to help readers organise and understand complex human behaviour through an integrated educational model.

They are **not** diagnostic instruments, validated clinical assessment tools, or standalone psychological theories.

Accountability Statement

Throughout this book, understanding behaviour is never presented as an excuse for harmful behaviour.

Understanding human systems helps explain how patterns develop.

Every individual remains responsible for the choices they make.

Safety, accountability, and the protection of children and families remain central principles throughout this work.

Publisher: Wolfpack Support Services

Edition: Wolfpack Edition

ISBN: 978-1-7648649-1-6

Contents

Dedication

For Every Child

For every child who learned to survive before they learned to feel safe.

For every adult carrying patterns they never chose.

For every parent determined to give their children something different.

For every practitioner, educator, first responder, and leader who refuses to accept violence as inevitable.

And for every person choosing to interrupt the ripple.

May the home become the place safety returns.

Disclaimer

A Note Before You Begin

This book discusses domestic and family violence, coercive control, trauma, emotional abuse, childhood adversity, and the lasting impact these experiences can have on individuals and families.

Some sections may be confronting.

If any part of this book feels overwhelming, give yourself permission to pause. Read at your own pace. Return when you feel ready.

If you are currently experiencing domestic or family violence, or believe someone you know may be at immediate risk, your first priority is safety. Please seek support from trusted services, emergency responders, or qualified professionals in your local area.

This book is not written to assign blame.

It is written to build understanding.

Understanding does not excuse harm.

Understanding helps prevent it.

About This Book

Why This Book Exists

Violence does not begin with violence.

Long before the first threat, the first insult, or the first act of physical harm, something far less visible has often been happening.

Pressure has been building.

Capacity has been shrinking.

Fear has been replacing trust.

Control has been replacing connection.

Choices have been reinforcing patterns.

Human systems have gradually lost the ability to maintain safety.

This book explores those systems.

Not to excuse violence.

Not to minimise accountability.

But because preventing harm requires us to understand how harm develops.

The Wolfpack Way approaches domestic and family violence through the lens of human systems.

It asks a different question.

Instead of asking:

"How do we respond after violence?"

It asks:

"How do we build homes where violence becomes less likely to emerge?"

Understanding human systems explains behaviour.

Accountability changes behaviour.

Both are necessary.

Scope of This Book

This book examines domestic and family violence through the lens of human systems.

It focuses on understanding how pressure, identity, emotional regulation, relationships, repeated choices, and capacity interact over time to shape the safety of families.

While no single framework can explain every circumstance, The Wolfpack Way provides an educational model for understanding how human systems function under pressure and how they can be strengthened before harm becomes normal.

This book is intended for adults, parents, educators, practitioners, leaders, and anyone committed to building safer families and stronger communities.

The Wolfpack Principle

Human Systems

Every human system exists in relationship with other human systems.

Individuals.

Couples.

Families.

Teams.

Schools.

Workplaces.

Communities.

Each system experiences pressure.

Each system has finite capacity.

When capacity exceeds pressure, people are more likely to respond with flexibility, connection, accountability, and emotional safety.

When pressure repeatedly exceeds capacity, survival strategies become increasingly likely.

Those strategies may protect in the short term.

If left unexamined, they can become harmful over time.

Human systems help explain behaviour.

They never remove responsibility.

How to Use This Book

This is not a book to rush.

Some chapters will explain.

Some will challenge.

Some may feel deeply personal.

You do not need to agree with everything immediately.

Allow yourself time to reflect.

Use the reflection questions.

Return to the diagrams.

Notice the patterns.

Most importantly, notice your own capacity as you read.

This book is not about finding broken people.

It is about understanding human systems.

The Commitment We Make Together

If you are reading this as a survivor, I hope this book helps you understand that what happened to you was never your fault, and that understanding the system that surrounded you is part of reclaiming your future.

If you are reading this because you recognise harmful patterns in yourself, I hope you have the courage to keep reading. Understanding those patterns is not the end of accountability. It is the beginning of it.

If you are reading this as a parent, partner, practitioner, teacher, leader, or community member, I hope this book helps you create spaces where safety grows instead of fear.

The purpose of this book is not to divide people into heroes and villains.

The purpose is to understand the human systems that shape behaviour so that more homes become places where children are loved, belong, know their worth, and never have to recover from the place that was meant to protect them.

Chapter 1

Every Human Begins With Three Questions

"The way we answer these questions quietly shapes the rest of our lives."

No human being enters the world asking to become anxious.

No child dreams of becoming controlling.

No teenager hopes to spend years believing they are not enough.

No adult wakes up one morning and decides they want to build relationships based on fear instead of trust.

Yet every day, human beings live lives shaped by patterns they never consciously chose.

Before we understand behaviour, we need to understand where behaviour begins.

Not with violence.

Not with anger.

Not with control.

Not even with trauma.

It begins much earlier.

It begins with three questions every human being is trying to answer.

Often without ever speaking them aloud.

Three Questions

Every child enters the world asking:

Am I loved?

Do I belong?

Do I have worth?

These questions are not philosophical.

They are biological.

Relational.

Developmental.

Every interaction begins teaching the nervous system something about these three questions.

A comforting hug.

A frightened parent.

An encouraging teacher.

An absent caregiver.

A sibling.

A grandparent.

A sporting coach.

A neighbourhood.

A family meal.

A slammed door.

Every experience becomes information.

Slowly, a human operating system begins to form.

We Learn Safety Before We Learn Language

Long before children understand words, they are learning safety.

They notice:

Who comes back.

Who doesn't.

Who comforts.

Who criticises.

Who listens.

Who shouts.

Who repairs.

Who withdraws.

Safety is experienced before it is explained.

Children do not need to understand conflict to be shaped by it.

They simply need to live inside it.

Human Systems Build Human Systems

No one develops in isolation.

Every human system develops inside another human system.

Families.

Schools.

Communities.

Culture.

Friendships.

Workplaces.

Relationships.

The environments around us become part of the environments within us.

The messages we repeatedly receive slowly become the messages we begin telling ourselves.

Over time they become beliefs.

Beliefs become identity.

Identity influences behaviour.

Behaviour creates ripples.

This is how human systems reproduce themselves across generations.

Not because people want suffering.

Because patterns become familiar.

And familiar often feels safer than unknown.

Capacity Begins Here

One of the greatest misunderstandings about behaviour is believing people simply choose to react the way they do.

Choice matters.

Accountability matters.

But every choice is made within a human system carrying a different amount of available capacity.

Capacity is our ability to remain present, flexible, thoughtful and connected while experiencing pressure.

Some people begin life with human systems that continually build capacity.

Others begin life inside systems that continually consume it.

Neither determines a person's future.

But both influence the starting point.

The First Lessons About Love

Children do not only learn whether they are loved.

They learn what love looks like.

If love feels safe...

They often learn connection.

If love feels unpredictable...

They may learn hypervigilance.

If love feels conditional...

They may learn performance.

If love feels absent...

They may learn self-reliance long before they are ready.

If love feels frightening...

They may learn that closeness and danger belong together.

These are not conscious decisions.

They are adaptive responses.

The human system is always trying to answer one question:

"What do I need to do to stay safe here?"

The Questions Never Leave

Most adults believe they stopped asking those three questions years ago.

In reality...

Many of us spend our entire lives answering them.

Some search for love through approval.

Some search for belonging through conformity.

Some search for worth through achievement.

Some search through control.

Some through perfection.

Some through pleasing everyone else.

Some through power.

Some through silence.

The strategy changes.

The questions remain.

This Book Is About Human Systems

This is not a book about broken people.

It is not a book about monsters.

It is not a book about reducing human behaviour to a single explanation.

It is a book about human systems.

Human systems under pressure.

Human systems trying to meet needs.

Human systems carrying stories.

Human systems making choices.

Human systems building safety.

Or slowly losing it.

Domestic and family violence does not emerge from nowhere.

It develops within human systems that have gradually become organised around fear, control and repeated harmful choices.

Understanding those systems does not excuse violence.

It gives us the opportunity to prevent more of it.

Reflection

Before continuing, pause for a moment.

Without judgement...

Ask yourself the same three questions.

Do I know that I am loved?

Do I feel that I truly belong?

Can I recognise my own worth without having to earn it?

There are no right answers.

Only honest ones.

Because every human system begins somewhere.

The rest of this book is about understanding where those beginnings can lead—and how they can change.

Chapter 2

The Human Operating System

"Before we understand behaviour, we must understand the system creating it."

Every person you have ever met has an operating system.

It cannot be downloaded.

It cannot be seen on a brain scan.

It cannot be measured with a single test.

Yet it quietly influences every conversation, every relationship, every decision, and every behaviour.

Most people never realise it exists.

They simply believe:

"This is just who I am."

But the person you became is not simply the person you were born to be.

You are also the product of thousands of experiences interacting with one another across your lifetime.

Your Human Operating System has been learning from the day you entered the world.

Every experience has added information.

Every relationship has taught lessons.

Every success has built confidence.

Every disappointment has shaped expectations.

Every environment has influenced what your nervous system believes is safe.

Over time those experiences became the system through which you now interpret the world.

Human Systems Learn

One of the greatest myths about behaviour is that people simply react to what is happening around them.

In reality, people respond to what their operating system believes is happening.

Two people can experience exactly the same event and respond completely differently.

One remains calm.

Another becomes overwhelmed.

One sees opportunity.

Another sees danger.

One asks questions.

Another prepares for conflict.

The difference is rarely the event itself.

The difference is the system interpreting the event.

Building the Operating System

Imagine your Human Operating System as a series of connected layers.

Every layer influences the next.

Your environment teaches experiences.

Experiences create meaning.

Meaning shapes beliefs.

Beliefs influence identity.

Identity influences needs.

Needs influence strategies.

Strategies become behaviours.

Behaviours create outcomes.

Outcomes reinforce the system.

Nothing exists in isolation.

Every part influences every other part.

This is why changing behaviour alone rarely creates lasting change.

If the operating system remains the same, the behaviour often returns.

The Human Hologram

The Human Hologram is the visual map of this operating system.

It helps us understand how seemingly unrelated parts of life connect.

Experiences.

Relationships.

Messages.

Biology.

Environment.

Identity.

Needs.

Capacity.

Behaviour.

Ripple.

Instead of asking only,

"Why did this person do that?"

the Human Hologram encourages a different question.

"What system produced this behaviour?"

That question does not remove responsibility.

It simply gives us more places to intervene before harm occurs.

Behaviour Is Information

Most people judge behaviour.

The Human Operating System studies behaviour.

Behaviour is not random.

Behaviour is information.

It tells us something about the interaction between pressure and capacity.

It tells us something about the needs a person is trying to meet.

It tells us something about the identity they are protecting.

It tells us something about the environments they have adapted to.

Behaviour is the visible part of a much larger system.

If we only react to behaviour, we often miss the forces creating it.

Capacity Is the Currency

Every human system has a finite amount of available capacity.

Capacity is the ability to remain present, flexible, emotionally regulated, and connected while experiencing pressure.

Capacity is constantly changing.

Sleep influences it.

Stress influences it.

Relationships influence it.

Health influences it.

Purpose influences it.

Connection influences it.

Loss influences it.

Recovery influences it.

Capacity is never fixed.

Some days we have plenty.

Other days we are already running on empty before the day begins.

Understanding capacity changes how we understand behaviour.

People are rarely operating from the same starting point.

Pressure Reveals the System

Pressure does not create character.

Pressure reveals the operating system already in place.

Under pressure, people often return to the strategies that have worked before.

Some become quiet.

Some become angry.

Some work harder.

Some withdraw.

Some seek reassurance.

Some seek control.

Some become helpers.

Some become critics.

These strategies are not random.

They were learned somewhere.

Repeated somewhere.

Reinforced somewhere.

The question is not whether we have survival strategies.

Every human being does.

The question is whether those strategies continue creating safety or have started creating harm.

Why Systems Matter

Most interventions focus on behaviour.

Stop shouting.

Stop controlling.

Stop avoiding.

Stop reacting.

Those are worthwhile goals.

But behaviour is often the final expression of a much larger system.

If we never strengthen the system, we spend our lives fighting symptoms.

Human systems allow us to work further upstream.

Where capacity can be built.

Needs can be met more effectively.

Identity can become more secure.

Relationships can become safer.

Behaviour changes because the system supporting it has changed.

The Foundation of This Book

Every chapter that follows returns to this operating system.

Sometimes we will focus on identity.

Sometimes capacity.

Sometimes needs.

Sometimes relationships.

Sometimes behaviour.

Sometimes the ripple that behaviour creates across generations.

Together they form one human system.

Domestic and family violence is not explained by one layer alone.

Neither is healing.

Neither is parenting.

Neither is leadership.

Neither is being human.

Understanding the whole system does not make change easy.

It makes change possible.

Reflection

Think about someone you know well.

Perhaps a parent.

A partner.

A friend.

A colleague.

Or yourself.

Instead of asking,

"What behaviour do I see?"

Ask,

"What human system might be producing that behaviour?"

You may discover that the answer is far more complex, and far more hopeful, than behaviour alone could ever reveal.

We do not become safer by controlling behaviour alone.

We become safer by strengthening the human systems that shape behaviour in the first place.

Chapter 3

Capacity Is the Missing Conversation

"Pressure does not affect everyone equally. The difference is often capacity."

Imagine placing the same weight into two different backpacks.

One backpack is empty.

The other is already full of bricks.

The weight is identical.

The experience is completely different.

Human beings work the same way.

Life does not distribute pressure evenly.

Nor do people carry it with the same amount of available capacity.

This is one of the greatest misunderstandings in conversations about behaviour.

We often judge what people do without asking how much pressure their system was already carrying.

Understanding capacity does not excuse behaviour.

It helps explain why the same event can produce very different responses.

What Is Capacity?

Capacity is your ability to remain emotionally present, flexible, thoughtful, and connected while experiencing pressure.

It is not toughness.

It is not intelligence.

It is not willpower.

Capacity is the available space within your human system to respond rather than simply react.

It changes every day.

Sometimes every hour.

Some experiences build capacity.

Others quietly consume it.

Most people never notice either happening.

Capacity Is Not Character

People often say,

"They just couldn't handle it."

That statement is usually interpreted as weakness.

The reality is often much more complex.

Capacity is influenced by countless interacting factors.

Sleep.

Health.

Stress.

Financial pressure.

Relationships.

Purpose.

Grief.

Nutrition.

Isolation.

Past experiences.

Recovery.

Support.

Meaning.

Hope.

No single factor determines capacity.

Every factor contributes to it.

This is why judging behaviour without understanding capacity often leads to simplistic conclusions.

Human Systems Carry Invisible Weight

Every person walks into every room carrying something invisible.

Some carry confidence.

Some carry exhaustion.

Some carry grief.

Some carry uncertainty.

Some carry unresolved trauma.

Some carry shame.

Some carry responsibility for everyone around them.

Others carry loneliness so familiar they no longer notice it.

The weight is invisible.

The capacity it consumes is not.

Pressure Is Neutral

Pressure is neither good nor bad.

Pressure helps children learn.

Pressure helps athletes improve.

Pressure helps leaders grow.

Pressure strengthens muscles.

Pressure develops resilience.

Pressure creates adaptation.

The problem is not pressure.

The problem is when pressure consistently exceeds the capacity available to carry it safely.

That is when survival begins replacing regulation.

What Happens When Capacity Runs Low?

As capacity decreases, the human system becomes increasingly focused on safety.

Thinking narrows.

Flexibility reduces.

Patience becomes harder.

Perspective shrinks.

Small frustrations feel larger.

Misunderstandings escalate more quickly.

Emotions become louder.

Recovery takes longer.

The nervous system is not trying to become difficult.

It is trying to preserve itself.

Capacity and Human Needs

When capacity is high, people are generally able to meet their needs through healthy, resourceful strategies.

Connection.

Communication.

Boundaries.

Contribution.

Learning.

Repair.

When capacity becomes depleted, immediate relief often becomes more attractive than long-term wellbeing.

Certainty may become more important than connection.

Control may feel safer than vulnerability.

Avoidance may feel easier than honesty.

Anger may feel more accessible than sadness.

The need itself is not the problem.

The strategy used to meet it often determines whether the outcome builds safety or creates harm.

The Capacity Bucket

Imagine every human being carries an invisible bucket.

Every day experiences either add to it or drain from it.

Rest adds.

Sleep adds.

Connection adds.

Purpose adds.

Movement adds.

Repair adds.

Hope adds.

Conflict drains.

Financial stress drains.

Poor health drains.

Isolation drains.

Fear drains.

Shame drains.

Uncertainty drains.

Loss drains.

Eventually one more drop causes the bucket to overflow.

Most people assume the final drop caused the reaction.

In reality, it simply arrived last.

Capacity and Family Safety

Families do not lose safety overnight.

Safety gradually erodes when capacity is repeatedly consumed faster than it can be restored.

Parents become overwhelmed.

Communication becomes reactive.

Repair becomes less frequent.

Conflict lasts longer.

Children adapt.

Partners withdraw.

Control slowly replaces collaboration.

Pressure keeps increasing.

Capacity keeps decreasing.

Unless something changes, the human system begins organising itself around survival rather than connection.

Why This Matters

This book is not asking,

"Why did someone become violent?"

It is asking,

"What happened within the human system before violence became possible?"

That question changes everything.

Because if we understand how capacity is built...

We can strengthen it.

If we understand how capacity is lost...

We can protect it.

If we understand how human systems organise themselves under pressure...

We can intervene much earlier.

That is where prevention begins.

Reflection

Think about your own capacity today.

Not yesterday.

Not last year.

Today.

What has been filling your bucket?

What has been emptying it?

Which pressures are temporary?

Which have become your normal?

Which parts of your life build capacity?

Which quietly consume it?

Awareness is not the end of change.

But it is often where change begins.

Families rarely lose safety because one difficult day occurred.

They lose safety when pressure continues to rise while capacity quietly disappears.

The earlier we recognise that imbalance, the greater our opportunity to build safety before survival begins organising the system.

Chapter 4

The Pressure We Were Never Designed to Carry

"Human systems were built to recover from pressure, not live inside it."

Pressure has always been part of being human.

Our ancestors faced drought.

Conflict.

Disease.

Predators.

Loss.

Uncertainty.

Pressure itself is not new.

What has changed is how long pressure now remains switched on.

Many human systems no longer experience moments of stress followed by recovery.

Instead, they experience constant activation.

Financial pressure.

Relationship pressure.

Parenting pressure.

Housing pressure.

Work pressure.

Technology pressure.

Social pressure.

The human operating system was built to adapt.

It was never designed to remain permanently overloaded.

The Difference Between Stress and Overload

Stress is not always harmful.

Stress can help us grow.

Learn.

Adapt.

Develop confidence.

Build resilience.

Overload is different.

Overload occurs when demands continue exceeding the available capacity to manage them.

Recovery becomes shorter.

Pressure becomes constant.

The nervous system stops asking,

"Is this stressful?"

Instead it begins asking,

"When will the next problem arrive?"

Living in that state changes the way human systems function.

Modern Life Consumes Capacity

Many people wake already exhausted.

Not because they are weak.

Because their capacity has already been consumed before the day begins.

Poor sleep.

Financial worries.

Relationship conflict.

Work deadlines.

School demands.

Family responsibilities.

Constant notifications.

Endless information.

News.

Emails.

Social media.

Traffic.

Bills.

Appointments.

Decision after decision.

Every demand draws from the same capacity reserve.

Most people are not carrying one heavy weight.

They are carrying hundreds of small ones.

Human Systems Need Recovery

Every healthy system follows a rhythm.

Effort.

Recovery.

Growth.

The human body understands this.

Muscles become stronger during recovery.

Learning consolidates during rest.

Relationships deepen through repair.

Emotions settle through regulation.

Capacity grows through restoration.

Without recovery, every system begins to deteriorate.

Human systems are no different.

The Illusion of Recovery

Many people believe they are recovering.

Often they are simply distracting themselves.

Scrolling.

Television.

Alcohol.

Gaming.

Shopping.

Overworking.

Constant busyness.

Distraction can reduce discomfort.

It rarely restores capacity.

Recovery is different.

Recovery reconnects us with ourselves.

Sleep.

Movement.

Connection.

Nature.

Purpose.

Stillness.

Meaning.

Repair.

Healthy relationships.

Recovery is not the absence of activity.

It is the rebuilding of capacity.

Pressure Changes Relationships

As capacity decreases, relationships often begin carrying the consequences.

Communication becomes shorter.

Patience becomes thinner.

Misunderstandings increase.

Repair becomes less frequent.

Small disagreements become larger conflicts.

Partners stop feeling heard.

Children stop feeling emotionally safe.

No one intended for this to happen.

The system gradually lost the capacity to respond differently.

That does not remove responsibility.

It explains why relationships often become the first place capacity shortages become visible.

The Weight of Multiple Roles

Modern adults rarely hold one identity.

Many hold several at once.

Partner.

Parent.

Employee.

Employer.

Carer.

Volunteer.

Coach.

Friend.

Adult child.

Community member.

Each role carries expectations.

Each expectation requires emotional energy.

Each responsibility consumes capacity.

The issue is rarely one role.

It is carrying too many without enough opportunity to recover.

Pressure Does Not Create Harm

Pressure alone does not create domestic and family violence.

Millions of people experience enormous pressure without becoming controlling or violent.

Pressure does not remove accountability.

Pressure simply increases the likelihood that existing survival strategies will emerge if healthier strategies have not been developed.

The question is never,

"Was life hard?"

The question is,

"When life became hard, what strategies did the human system rely upon?"

That is where accountability begins.

The Human System Under Chronic Pressure

When pressure remains high for long periods, human systems often begin adapting.

Attention narrows.

Threat becomes easier to detect.

Flexibility decreases.

Certainty becomes increasingly valuable.

Control can begin feeling safer than uncertainty.

Immediate relief becomes more attractive than long-term growth.

These adaptations make sense inside survival.

The problem begins when survival becomes the normal way of living.

Why Prevention Starts Here

Most prevention begins after the crisis.

The Wolfpack Way begins before it.

Before the argument.

Before the withdrawal.

Before the intimidation.

Before the control.

Before the violence.

It begins by asking a different question.

"What is consuming this human system's capacity?"

That question does not solve every problem.

But it often reveals problems while they are still small enough to change.

Reflection

Think about your own life.

Not your behaviour.

Your pressure.

What has become normal that should not have become normal?

Where are you constantly giving energy without replacing it?

Which responsibilities build your capacity?

Which responsibilities quietly drain it?

If someone looked only at your behaviour, what invisible pressures would they never see?

Human systems rarely fail because they experience pressure.

They fail when pressure becomes constant and recovery becomes rare.

Every effort to build safer families begins by protecting the capacity that allows people to choose connection instead of survival.

Chapter 5

The Survival Identity

"Long before behaviour becomes visible, identity has often already adapted."

Every human being is born with the capacity to grow, connect, explore, and belong.

Children are naturally curious.

They seek closeness.

They look for safety.

They learn through relationship.

They do not enter the world believing they are broken.

They learn who they need to become from the environments around them.

Sometimes those lessons support healthy development.

Sometimes they support survival.

There is a difference.

We Adapt Before We Understand

Children do not analyse their environment.

They adapt to it.

If home feels calm, they learn calm.

If home feels unpredictable, they learn vigilance.

If love feels conditional, they learn performance.

If anger feels dangerous, they learn silence.

If conflict feels unavoidable, they learn protection.

These adaptations are not signs of weakness.

They are evidence that the human operating system is doing exactly what it was designed to do.

Survive.

Identity Is More Than Personality

Many people think identity is simply who they are.

The Human Operating System sees identity differently.

Identity is the story your human system tells about who you must become to remain safe, connected, or valued.

Some people become the achiever.

Some become the helper.

Some become invisible.

Some become the protector.

Some become the peacemaker.

Some become the controller.

Some become the rebel.

Each identity once solved a problem.

The question is whether it still serves the life you are trying to build today.

The Birth of the Survival Identity

Every adaptation begins with a lesson.

"I need to be perfect."

"I must never cry."

"I have to keep everyone happy."

"I cannot trust anyone."

"I have to stay in control."

"If I disappoint people, I will be abandoned."

These lessons are rarely taught directly.

They are learned through repetition.

Eventually they stop feeling like beliefs.

They begin feeling like truth.

The survival identity is born.

Identity Protects What It Believes Is Necessary

Once identity forms, it begins protecting itself.

If your identity says,

"I must always be strong,"

showing vulnerability feels dangerous.

If your identity says,

"I am responsible for everyone,"

rest becomes guilt.

If your identity says,

"I am only valuable when I achieve,"

failure becomes a threat to your worth.

The human system is not protecting reality.

It is protecting the identity that once helped it survive.

The Identity and Needs Loop

Identity and human needs constantly influence one another.

The identity tells the system which needs matter most.

Those needs then drive behaviour.

Behaviour temporarily satisfies the need.

The identity feels confirmed.

The loop continues.

For example:

A child grows up believing,

"I am only noticed when I perform."

As an adult, significance becomes a dominant need.

Achievement becomes the strategy.

Success briefly provides relief.

The identity says,

"See? This is who we have to be."

The cycle repeats.

The behaviour is reinforced.

Not because it creates lasting wellbeing.

Because it temporarily protects the identity.

When Healthy Needs Become Harmful Strategies

Every human need is legitimate.

The problem is rarely the need itself.

The problem is how the need is being met.

A need for certainty can become healthy routines.

Or it can become controlling another person.

A need for belonging can become genuine connection.

Or it can become abandoning yourself to keep everyone else happy.

A need for significance can become meaningful contribution.

Or it can become domination and power.

The need is not the danger.

The strategy determines whether safety grows or disappears.

Identity Under Pressure

Pressure does not create a survival identity.

Pressure reveals it.

When capacity is high, people can choose flexible responses.

When capacity becomes depleted, the human system often returns to familiar survival strategies.

The achiever works harder.

The people pleaser sacrifices more.

The controller tightens control.

The avoider disappears.

The rescuer forgets themselves.

The critic attacks.

These responses are predictable because the identity has rehearsed them for years.

Why This Matters for Families

No family begins by wanting fear to replace safety.

No relationship begins hoping control will replace trust.

These changes occur gradually.

As pressure rises and capacity falls, survival identities begin leading the system.

One partner may pursue certainty through control.

Another may pursue belonging through self-sacrifice.

Another may pursue safety through silence.

Each person believes they are protecting something important.

Without awareness and accountability, those strategies slowly reshape the relationship itself.

Survival Is Not the Enemy

The survival identity deserves respect.

It helped you get here.

It protected you when healthier options may not have existed.

But survival was never designed to become your permanent identity.

There comes a point where the strategies that once protected you begin limiting you.

Healing is not about hating your survival identity.

Healing is about thanking it for its service while recognising it no longer has to lead your life.

Reflection

Think about your own life.

When you feel under pressure, who do you become?

Do you become the achiever?

The helper?

The peacemaker?

The protector?

The controller?

The invisible one?

The critic?

The rescuer?

Ask yourself one more question.

When did that version of you first become necessary?

You may discover that the answer has very little to do with today.

Human beings rarely protect behaviours.

They protect identities.

When identity feels threatened, behaviour often becomes an attempt to preserve the person we believe we must be.

Real change begins when we realise we no longer have to survive the life we are living.

Chapter 6

The Identity and Needs Loop

"Human beings rarely repeat behaviours because they enjoy suffering. They repeat behaviours because those behaviours continue meeting an important need."

One of the biggest mistakes we make is believing behaviour exists on its own.

It does not.

Every behaviour serves a purpose.

Every behaviour attempts to solve a problem.

Every behaviour meets a need.

The question is never simply,

"Why did they behave like that?"

The deeper question is,

"What need was the human system attempting to meet?"

Until we understand that question, lasting change remains difficult.

Because removing behaviour without understanding the need usually creates replacement behaviour.

The need never disappeared.

Only the strategy changed.

Human Needs Drive Human Behaviour

Every human being has psychological needs.

We need certainty.

We need uncertainty and growth.

We need connection.

We need significance.

We need purpose.

We need contribution.

These needs are not good or bad.

They are simply part of being human.

The Human Operating System is constantly trying to balance them.

When they are met in healthy ways, people often become more flexible, connected and emotionally safe.

When they are repeatedly unmet, the system searches for another strategy.

Identity Chooses Which Need Matters Most

Not every need becomes equally important.

Identity decides which needs become non-negotiable.

A child who grows up in chaos may place certainty above everything else.

A child who felt invisible may organise life around significance.

A child who feared abandonment may chase connection at any cost.

A child who carried adult responsibilities may struggle to receive support because contribution became part of identity.

The need is not random.

It reflects the story the human system learned about survival.

The Identity and Needs Loop

Every human system follows a loop.

Experiences shape identity.

Identity prioritises certain needs.

Needs drive strategies.

Strategies produce behaviours.

Behaviours temporarily satisfy needs.

The identity feels confirmed.

The cycle repeats.

Over time, repetition strengthens the loop.

Eventually the behaviour no longer feels like a choice.

It feels like who we are.

When Healthy Needs Find Harmful Strategies

Every psychological need can be met in many different ways.

A need for certainty may become healthy routines and trustworthy relationships.

Or it may become rigid control over another person.

A need for significance may become meaningful contribution.

Or it may become intimidation, dominance or power.

A need for connection may become secure attachment.

Or it may become people pleasing, dependency or abandoning yourself to avoid rejection.

A need for growth may become learning.

Or it may become chasing constant stimulation without reflection.

The need is never the enemy.

The strategy determines whether the human system becomes healthier or more harmful.

Why Harmful Patterns Feel So Difficult to Change

People often ask,

"If this behaviour causes so much pain, why doesn't it stop?"

Because stopping the behaviour often feels like losing the only strategy the identity trusts.

Imagine someone whose identity says,

"I am only safe when I remain in control."

Removing controlling behaviour does not immediately create safety.

It creates uncertainty.

The identity experiences that uncertainty as danger.

Without developing healthier ways to meet the need for certainty, the human system naturally attempts to return to familiar strategies.

This is why lasting change requires more than insight.

It requires new experiences that teach the operating system a different way of meeting the same need.

Human Systems Under Pressure

When capacity is high, people usually have more options.

They can pause.

Reflect.

Repair.

Negotiate.

Compromise.

When capacity becomes depleted, the operating system becomes increasingly focused on immediate need fulfilment.

Long-term thinking gives way to short-term relief.

Connection gives way to certainty.

Flexibility gives way to rigidity.

Curiosity gives way to protection.

This is not because the need changed.

It is because capacity reduced the number of strategies the system believed were available.

Families Develop Shared Loops

Needs do not exist only within individuals.

Families develop shared patterns.

One person seeks certainty through control.

Another seeks belonging through compliance.

Another seeks significance through achievement.

Children observe these strategies.

They adapt.

Eventually the family's way of meeting needs begins shaping the next generation's operating system.

Without awareness, the loop continues.

Not because anyone wanted it to.

Because it became familiar.

Breaking the Loop

Lasting change rarely begins by asking,

"How do I stop this behaviour?"

A more powerful question is,

"What need is this behaviour trying to meet?"

The next question follows naturally.

"What healthier strategy could meet that same need without creating harm?"

This is where regulation becomes possible.

This is where accountability becomes possible.

This is where growth begins.

The Difference Between Relief and Healing

Relief is immediate.

Healing is intentional.

Relief reduces discomfort for a moment.

Healing builds capacity for a lifetime.

Control may create temporary certainty.

Connection creates lasting safety.

Avoidance may reduce fear today.

Courage builds confidence tomorrow.

People pleasing may reduce conflict.

Boundaries build healthier relationships.

The operating system does not need fewer needs.

It needs healthier strategies.

Reflection

Think about one behaviour you repeat when life becomes difficult.

Ask yourself three questions.

What need is this behaviour trying to meet?

What identity is it protecting?

What healthier strategy could meet the same need without creating harm?

The answer may reveal far more than the behaviour itself ever could.

Human behaviour is rarely random.

It is often the operating system's best attempt to meet an important need using the strategies it currently trusts.

Healing begins when we stop asking people to abandon their needs and start helping them discover healthier ways to meet them.

Chapter 7

When Safety Begins to Leave

"Relationships rarely become unsafe overnight. They change one pattern at a time."

Very few relationships begin with fear.

Most begin with hope.

Connection.

Trust.

Curiosity.

Shared dreams.

The desire to build a life together.

No one stands at an altar hoping to create an emotionally unsafe home.

No one starts a family planning to build fear instead of security.

Human systems rarely change all at once.

They change gradually.

The challenge is that gradual change is difficult to notice while living inside it.

Safety Is More Than Physical

When people hear the word "safety," many think only about physical harm.

Physical safety matters.

It always matters.

But emotional safety often disappears long before physical violence appears.

Emotional safety means feeling able to speak honestly without fear.

To make mistakes without humiliation.

To disagree without punishment.

To express emotion without ridicule.

To remain yourself without losing connection.

When emotional safety weakens, relationships begin reorganising around protection rather than trust.

The Shift Is Usually Subtle

Safety rarely disappears in one moment.

It often leaves quietly.

Conversations become shorter.

Repair happens less often.

Apologies disappear.

Criticism becomes more common.

Walking on eggshells becomes normal.

One person begins changing their behaviour to avoid another person's reaction.

Not because they want to.

Because the human system adapts.

Adaptation is what human systems do.

Fear Changes the Operating System

Fear reorganises attention.

People begin watching tone instead of listening to words.

They monitor facial expressions.

Footsteps.

Text messages.

The sound of a car pulling into the driveway.

Silence.

The atmosphere in the room.

Their operating system stops asking,

"What do I want?"

It begins asking,

"What keeps me safe right now?"

This is survival.

Relationships Become Predictable

As safety reduces, relationships often become organised around predictable roles.

One pursues.

One withdraws.

One controls.

One accommodates.

One criticises.

One apologises.

One carries responsibility.

One carries fear.

These roles may change over time.

But once established, they often reinforce one another.

Without intervention, the relationship becomes organised around surviving each other instead of supporting each other.

Adaptation Is Not the Same as Safety

One of the greatest misconceptions is believing that because a relationship continues functioning, it must be healthy.

Human systems are remarkably adaptable.

People learn to avoid topics.

Avoid conflict.

Avoid asking for help.

Avoid expressing emotion.

Avoid disagreeing.

The relationship continues.

From the outside, everything appears normal.

Inside, safety has already begun leaving.

Functioning is not always the same as flourishing.

The Cost of Living in Survival

When relationships become organised around survival, everyone begins paying a price.

Communication becomes defensive.

Trust becomes fragile.

Children notice more than adults realise.

Joy becomes less frequent.

Laughter becomes cautious.

Curiosity becomes suspicion.

Connection becomes management.

The relationship may continue for years.

But the human system slowly forgets what genuine emotional safety feels like.

The First Warning Signs

Most unsafe relationships do not begin with violence.

They begin with repeated patterns.

Fear of speaking honestly.

Needing permission for ordinary decisions.

Feeling responsible for another person's emotional state.

Constant criticism.

Isolation from family or friends.

Walking on eggshells.

Monitoring moods.

Changing your behaviour to prevent another person's reaction.

Believing peace depends entirely on keeping someone else calm.

These patterns deserve attention.

Not because they prove violence will occur.

Because they tell us safety is already changing.

Why Early Recognition Matters

The earlier human systems recognise the loss of safety, the greater the opportunity to intervene.

Not every struggling relationship becomes abusive.

Not every conflict becomes coercion.

But every emotionally safe relationship depends upon the ability to repair, communicate, respect boundaries, and remain accountable.

When those foundations begin disappearing, intervention becomes increasingly important.

The goal is never simply keeping relationships together.

The goal is protecting safety.

The Turning Point

This chapter marks a turning point in the book.

Until now, we have explored the human operating system.

From this point forward, we begin exploring what happens when multiple human systems interact under sustained pressure.

Because domestic and family violence is never experienced by one operating system alone.

It affects partners.

Children.

Extended families.

Communities.

Generations.

To understand family violence, we must first understand what happens when safety quietly leaves the relationship long before violence enters the room.

Reflection

Think about a relationship that has felt emotionally safe.

What made it feel safe?

Now think about a relationship that felt emotionally unsafe.

What changed first?

Was it shouting?

Or had safety already been disappearing long before anyone raised their voice?

Sometimes the most important changes are the ones no one else can see.

Violence rarely arrives without warning.

Long before physical harm, human systems often begin adapting to the gradual loss of emotional safety.

The earlier we recognise those changes, the greater our opportunity to protect people before fear becomes normal and control replaces connection.

Chapter 8

When Fear Becomes Control

"Control often begins where emotional safety has already been lost."

Control is one of the most misunderstood behaviours in human relationships.

People often imagine control as obvious.

Threats.

Orders.

Aggression.

Domination.

Sometimes it looks exactly like that.

More often, it does not.

Control frequently begins quietly.

It grows through repeated patterns that slowly reduce another person's freedom, confidence and emotional safety.

By the time control becomes obvious, the relationship has often been reorganising around fear for a long time.

Fear Seeks Certainty

The human operating system does not enjoy uncertainty.

When capacity is healthy, people can tolerate uncertainty.

They ask questions.

They negotiate.

They adapt.

When capacity is depleted and identity feels threatened, certainty becomes increasingly important.

Sometimes certainty is pursued through healthy strategies.

Planning.

Communication.

Boundaries.

Problem solving.

Sometimes certainty is pursued through unhealthy strategies.

Monitoring.

Checking.

Restricting.

Demanding.

Threatening.

Controlling.

The need is still certainty.

The strategy has changed.

The Difference Between Influence and Control

Healthy relationships influence each other.

They listen.

Compromise.

Respect differences.

Accept boundaries.

Control is different.

Control attempts to reduce another person's choices.

It replaces mutual respect with power.

Instead of asking,

"How do we solve this together?"

Control asks,

"How do I make sure this never happens again?"

One builds trust.

The other builds fear.

Control Is About Power

Many controlling behaviours are not about anger.

They are about power.

Who decides?

Who speaks?

Who apologises?

Who has access to money?

Who is allowed to see friends?

Who controls the timetable?

Who controls the children?

Who controls the information?

Control slowly shifts decision-making away from one person and concentrates it in another.

As power becomes unequal, safety begins disappearing.

The Slow Expansion of Control

Control rarely appears all at once.

It often expands gradually.

At first it may sound protective.

"I just worry about you."

Then it becomes limiting.

"I don't like you spending time with them."

Then it becomes monitoring.

"Tell me where you are."

Then it becomes demanding.

"Show me your phone."

Eventually the relationship is no longer built on trust.

It is built on permission.

The change often happens so gradually that both people adapt to it.

Human Systems Adapt to Control

One of the most important things to understand is this.

People adapt.

When someone lives inside a controlling relationship, they often begin making smaller and smaller adjustments.

Avoiding certain topics.

Changing how they dress.

Changing who they see.

Changing what they say.

Changing how they spend money.

Changing how they think.

Not because they have stopped caring about themselves.

Because the operating system has learned that adapting reduces immediate danger.

Adaptation is not agreement.

It is survival.

Control Does Not Require Violence

One of the greatest myths is that relationships are safe until physical violence occurs.

Many people live inside relationships where emotional safety disappeared years before anyone was physically harmed.

Control can exist through words.

Money.

Technology.

Isolation.

Humiliation.

Intimidation.

Threats.

Children.

Silence.

The absence of physical violence does not automatically mean the presence of emotional safety.

Children Learn Control Too

Children are always watching.

Not just behaviour.

Patterns.

They notice who makes decisions.

Who apologises.

Who withdraws.

Who becomes frightened.

Who carries responsibility.

Who controls the atmosphere in the home.

Children do not simply remember what parents say.

They learn what relationships feel like.

Without intervention, these experiences can become part of the next generation's Human Operating System.

Accountability Remains Central

Nothing in this chapter removes responsibility.

Many people experience fear without attempting to control others.

Many people experience uncertainty without becoming abusive.

Fear explains why the need for certainty may become stronger.

It does not justify controlling another human being.

Control is a choice.

Repeated control is a pattern.

Patterns can change.

Only when the person choosing them accepts responsibility for changing them.

Rebuilding Safety

Control cannot create genuine safety.

It can only create temporary compliance.

Real safety grows differently.

Through trust.

Respect.

Boundaries.

Repair.

Shared decision-making.

Emotional honesty.

Accountability.

Freedom.

The goal is not to control another person's behaviour.

The goal is to build a relationship where control is no longer necessary because safety exists.

Reflection

Think about the relationships in your own life.

Do people feel free to disagree with you?

Do you feel free to disagree with them?

Can mistakes be discussed without fear?

Can boundaries be respected without punishment?

Can people remain themselves without losing connection?

Those questions reveal far more about safety than conflict ever will.

Control is often the operating system's attempt to create certainty when it no longer trusts connection.

But certainty created through fear is never the same as safety created through trust.

One demands compliance.

The other allows people to remain fully human.

Chapter 9

When Control Becomes Harm

"The moment another person's freedom begins shrinking, safety is already being lost."

Control becomes harmful when it repeatedly removes another person's freedom, dignity, autonomy or sense of safety.

Not every disagreement is abuse.

Not every argument is coercion.

Not every mistake creates an unsafe relationship.

Healthy relationships experience conflict.

Healthy relationships experience frustration.

Healthy relationships make mistakes.

The difference is what happens next.

Healthy relationships repair.

Unsafe relationships increasingly rely on fear, intimidation, isolation and control.

The goal is no longer connection.

The goal becomes compliance.

Harm Is About Patterns

One difficult day does not define a relationship.

One argument does not define abuse.

One mistake does not define a person.

Patterns do.

Patterns reveal how a human system repeatedly responds when under pressure.

When control becomes the preferred strategy for managing fear, conflict or uncertainty, harm often begins expanding beyond isolated incidents.

It becomes the culture of the relationship.

Harm Takes Many Forms

Many people imagine domestic and family violence as physical assault.

Physical violence is one form of harm.

It is not the only one.

Relationships can become unsafe through repeated emotional abuse.

Financial control.

Social isolation.

Technology-facilitated monitoring.

Sexual coercion.

Threats.

Intimidation.

Property damage.

Using children to create fear or compliance.

Destroying confidence.

Undermining independence.

Controlling movement.

Controlling communication.

Controlling access to support.

Different behaviours.

One common outcome.

Reduced freedom.

Reduced safety.

Reduced autonomy.

Emotional Safety Is Often Lost First

Long before bruises become visible, emotional safety has often disappeared.

People stop expressing opinions.

Stop making independent decisions.

Stop seeing friends.

Stop speaking honestly.

Stop trusting their own judgement.

Many begin questioning themselves.

"Maybe I am overreacting."

"Maybe it really is my fault."

"Maybe I deserve this."

The operating system gradually reorganises around avoiding conflict rather than living freely.

Coercive Control

Coercive control is not one behaviour.

It is a repeated pattern of behaviours designed to dominate another person's everyday life.

The behaviours may appear small when viewed individually.

Together they create a system where freedom slowly disappears.

Everyday decisions become monitored.

Normal activities require permission.

Fear replaces confidence.

Isolation replaces connection.

Dependence replaces autonomy.

Control becomes the environment.

Not simply the behaviour.

Technology Changes the Landscape

Modern technology has created new ways to extend control.

Phones.

Location sharing.

Passwords.

Social media.

Banking applications.

Smart devices.

Messages.

Photos.

Digital monitoring.

Technology itself is neutral.

Human systems decide how it is used.

When technology becomes another tool for surveillance, intimidation or restriction, emotional safety continues shrinking even when the controlling person is not physically present.

Financial Control

Money influences freedom.

Healthy relationships discuss finances.

Plan together.

Share responsibility.

Respect independence.

Financial abuse is different.

It limits another person's ability to make choices.

Work.

Leave.

Travel.

Purchase essentials.

Access accounts.

Build independence.

Financial dependence often becomes another mechanism through which fear remains effective.

Children Live Inside the Pattern

Children do not simply witness harmful relationships.

They organise themselves around them.

Some become invisible.

Some become protectors.

Some become perfectionists.

Some become caretakers.

Some become aggressive.

Some become frightened.

Some learn to predict moods before they happen.

Children rarely understand the language of coercive control.

They understand the feeling.

The atmosphere.

The unpredictability.

The fear.

These experiences become part of their Human Operating System unless something interrupts the pattern.

Understanding Never Excuses Harm

This book has explored pressure.

Capacity.

Identity.

Needs.

Relationships.

Fear.

Control.

None of those concepts excuse abuse.

Understanding explains how harmful patterns may develop.

Accountability determines whether those patterns continue.

Every adult remains responsible for the choices they make.

Every person deserves relationships built upon safety rather than fear.

Understanding and accountability are partners.

Neither can replace the other.

Safety Must Come First

Whenever control becomes harm, safety becomes the priority.

Not preserving the relationship.

Not protecting appearances.

Not avoiding embarrassment.

Safety.

Sometimes that means boundaries.

Sometimes separation.

Sometimes legal intervention.

Sometimes specialist support.

Every situation is different.

One principle remains the same.

Human safety always comes before preserving unhealthy systems.

Reflection

Think beyond physical violence.

Consider emotional safety.

Can people disagree without fear?

Can they keep friendships?

Can they access money?

Can they make everyday decisions?

Can they express opinions without punishment?

Can they remain themselves?

If the answer repeatedly becomes no, the relationship deserves careful attention.

Control becomes harm when another person's freedom begins disappearing.

The goal of healthy relationships is never obedience.

It is mutual safety, mutual respect and shared responsibility.

Where fear replaces freedom, intervention becomes essential.

Chapter 10

The Children Who Inherit the System

"Children do not inherit only their family's genetics. They inherit its patterns, its atmosphere, and its understanding of safety."

Children do not choose the human systems they are born into.

They do not choose the emotional climate of their home.

They do not choose whether conflict is resolved through repair or fear.

They do not choose whether adults regulate themselves or expect children to regulate the room.

Yet every day, children adapt to the environment surrounding them.

That adaptation is one of the most extraordinary strengths of the human operating system.

It is also one of its greatest vulnerabilities.

Children Learn the Atmosphere

Adults often remember conversations.

Children remember atmosphere.

They remember how home felt.

Whether laughter was safe.

Whether silence meant danger.

Whether footsteps created relief or fear.

Whether mistakes were met with curiosity or criticism.

Whether adults repaired after conflict or pretended nothing happened.

The emotional atmosphere of a home quietly becomes part of a child's operating system.

Children Do Not Watch. They Participate.

One of the biggest misconceptions is that children simply witness domestic and family violence.

They do not.

They live inside it.

They organise their behaviour around it.

They learn when to speak.

When to stay quiet.

When to hide.

When to intervene.

When to comfort.

When to disappear.

Their nervous system is not observing the environment.

It is adapting to it.

The Roles Children Create

Children are remarkably creative in finding ways to survive.

Some become the invisible child.

"If nobody notices me, I will be safe."

Some become the peacemaker.

"If I keep everyone happy, maybe the fighting will stop."

Some become the achiever.

"If I perform well enough, perhaps everything will be okay."

Some become the protector.

"I have to look after Mum."

"I have to protect my brothers and sisters."

Some become the comedian.

"If I can make people laugh, maybe the tension will disappear."

Some become hypervigilant.

Always watching.

Always scanning.

Always preparing.

None of these roles begin as personality.

They begin as adaptation.

The Cost of Growing Up Too Soon

Many children living inside unsafe human systems become adults long before they should.

They learn responsibility before play.

Protection before exploration.

Monitoring before curiosity.

Helping before asking for help.

They become emotionally older than their years.

From the outside, they often appear mature.

Inside, many are carrying responsibilities no child was ever meant to carry.

The Nervous System Remembers

Children do not always remember every event.

Their nervous system remembers the feeling.

The tension.

The unpredictability.

The fear.

The relief.

The anticipation.

Years later they may struggle to explain why certain situations feel unsafe.

Their body learned the lesson before their mind could understand it.

The operating system remembers what words cannot always describe.

The Ripple Across Generations

Human systems naturally reproduce themselves.

Not because people want suffering.

Because familiarity often feels safer than uncertainty.

A child who grows up believing love requires self-sacrifice may unknowingly repeat that pattern.

A child who grows up believing control equals protection may carry that belief into adulthood.

A child who never experiences healthy repair may never learn what repair looks like.

The ripple is rarely intentional.

It is educational.

Children become students of the systems that raise them.

Not Every Child Repeats the Pattern

It is important to say this clearly.

Growing up inside an unsafe home does not determine a child's future.

Many people interrupt the ripple.

Many seek help.

Many build healthy relationships.

Many become deeply compassionate parents.

Many refuse to repeat what they experienced.

Human systems influence.

They do not imprison.

Every generation has the opportunity to choose differently.

The Adult Child

Years later, many adults still carry adaptations they first developed in childhood.

People pleasing.

Hypervigilance.

Perfectionism.

Emotional shutdown.

Difficulty trusting.

Difficulty resting.

Difficulty receiving love.

Difficulty believing they are worthy without performing.

These are not signs that someone is broken.

They are signs that their operating system once adapted to keep them safe.

The question becomes,

"Does this strategy still serve the life I am living today?"

The Greatest Gift We Give Children

Children do not need perfect parents.

They need emotionally safe human systems.

Adults who repair.

Adults who apologise.

Adults who regulate themselves.

Adults who model boundaries.

Adults who create predictable safety.

Children rarely need perfection.

They need enough safety to know that mistakes do not threaten love.

Reflection

Think back to your childhood.

Not the events.

The atmosphere.

How did home feel?

Who carried the emotional responsibility?

What role did you learn to play?

Does that role still appear in your relationships today?

Awareness is not about blaming the past.

It is about understanding what your operating system learned.

Children inherit far more than a family name.

They inherit the emotional operating system of the home they grow up inside.

The greatest legacy we leave is not what we own.

It is the safety our children experience while they are becoming themselves.

Chapter 11

The Adult the Child Becomes

"Children eventually grow up. Their operating systems come with them."

Children do not stay children forever.

They become partners.

Parents.

Friends.

Leaders.

Teachers.

Employers.

Employees.

Neighbours.

Community members.

One day the child who learned how to survive becomes the adult responsible for creating safety.

The question is not whether childhood matters.

The question is whether the patterns learned in childhood remain unexamined.

Because what remains unexamined often becomes repeated.

The Child Never Completely Leaves

Many adults believe childhood is over.

The calendar agrees.

The operating system often does not.

The child who learned that love had to be earned may still seek approval.

The child who never felt safe may still scan every room for danger.

The child who became responsible for everyone else may still struggle to rest.

The child who learned conflict meant fear may still avoid difficult conversations.

We often call these personality traits.

Sometimes they are survival strategies that simply grew older.

Yesterday Quietly Shapes Today

Most adults do not wake up intending to repeat painful patterns.

They wake up trying to build a better life.

Yet under pressure, familiar strategies often return.

Not because people want suffering.

Because familiar strategies require less conscious effort than unfamiliar ones.

The operating system trusts what it has practised.

Even when those strategies no longer create the life we want.

The Adult Operating System

As adults, our operating system influences nearly every important area of life.

How we love.

How we argue.

How we parent.

How we lead.

How we spend money.

How we respond to stress.

How we trust.

How we apologise.

How we repair.

How we recover.

Many people spend years trying to change behaviour while never examining the operating system producing it.

Relationships Reveal the Operating System

Few environments reveal our operating system more quickly than intimate relationships.

Partners experience our strengths.

Our fears.

Our needs.

Our habits.

Our blind spots.

Our survival strategies.

Relationships do not create the operating system.

They reveal it.

Pressure simply makes it easier to see.

Parenting Reveals the Next Layer

Children do not create our wounds.

They often expose them.

A crying child.

A defiant teenager.

A tired parent.

A stressful week.

These moments do not create survival strategies.

They reveal the strategies already living inside the adult.

This is why parenting can become one of the greatest opportunities for healing.

Children ask us to become the adult we may never have experienced ourselves.

Leadership Is No Different

The same operating system appears at work.

Under pressure, leaders often return to familiar strategies.

Some become controlling.

Some avoid difficult conversations.

Some overwork.

Some rescue.

Some criticise.

Some withdraw.

Leadership does not replace the operating system.

It magnifies it.

The greater the responsibility, the more visible the system becomes.

The Ripple Continues

Every adult influences other human systems.

Partners.

Children.

Teams.

Friendships.

Communities.

Every interaction teaches something.

Safety.

Fear.

Respect.

Control.

Repair.

Avoidance.

Accountability.

The question is never whether we create ripples.

We all do.

The question is which ripples we are creating.

Awareness Creates Choice

This is where hope begins.

The operating system can change.

Not overnight.

Not through insight alone.

Through awareness.

Practice.

Accountability.

New experiences.

Healthy relationships.

Repair.

Repeated choices.

Every time we choose a healthier response, the operating system receives new information.

Change is rarely dramatic.

It is usually built through repetition.

Breaking the Generational Loop

Many adults believe they must become the opposite of their parents.

The goal is not simply becoming different.

The goal is becoming intentional.

Some people repeat the past.

Some spend their lives running from it.

Healing allows us to do something different.

To choose what deserves to continue.

And leave behind what no longer serves future generations.

Every Adult Teaches Something

Whether we realise it or not, people are learning from us.

Children are learning.

Partners are learning.

Colleagues are learning.

Communities are learning.

Every human system teaches.

Not only through words.

Through behaviour.

Through consistency.

Through repair.

Through accountability.

Through emotional safety.

The question is simple.

"What is my operating system teaching the people around me?"

Reflection

Think about the adult you have become.

Which parts of you were intentionally chosen?

Which parts simply arrived through repetition?

Which survival strategies still appear when life becomes difficult?

Which strengths came from your experiences?

Which patterns deserve to end with you?

Awareness is not about blaming your past.

It is about accepting responsibility for your future.

Children become adults.

Adults become environments.

Those environments shape the next generation of children.

The ripple continues until someone becomes aware enough, courageous enough, and accountable enough to change its direction.

Chapter 12

Rebuilding the Human System

"Healing is not about becoming someone new. It is about building a human system that no longer needs survival to feel safe."

If human systems can learn fear, they can learn safety.

If they can learn control, they can learn trust.

If they can learn survival, they can learn regulation.

That does not mean change is easy.

It does not happen because someone reads a book.

Or attends one workshop.

Or makes one promise.

Human systems are built through repetition.

They are rebuilt the same way.

One experience.

One choice.

One repair.

One relationship.

One day at a time.

Awareness Opens the Door

The first step is awareness.

Not blame.

Not shame.

Awareness.

Most people cannot change patterns they cannot see.

That is why understanding the Human Operating System matters.

When you understand how your system was built, you gain the opportunity to choose how it continues developing.

Awareness is not the destination.

It is the doorway.

Responsibility Creates Movement

There is an important difference between explanation and responsibility.

Your past explains many things.

It does not decide your future.

At some point every adult reaches a moment where they must ask,

"What am I going to do with the operating system I have inherited?"

That question belongs to all of us.

Regardless of our childhood.

Regardless of our experiences.

Regardless of what happened before today.

Responsibility is where the ripple begins changing direction.

Capacity Must Be Rebuilt

Many people try to change behaviour while ignoring capacity.

Eventually they become exhausted.

Old strategies return.

The operating system goes back to what it trusts.

Real change begins by strengthening the foundation.

Sleep.

Movement.

Healthy relationships.

Meaningful work.

Recovery.

Nutrition.

Boundaries.

Purpose.

Emotional regulation.

Connection.

Capacity creates options.

Without capacity, survival strategies become increasingly attractive.

New Experiences Rewrite Old Expectations

The operating system learns through experience.

Not theory.

A person who grows up believing conflict always leads to danger needs repeated experiences of conflict ending with repair.

A person who believes vulnerability leads to rejection needs repeated experiences of being accepted while remaining authentic.

A person who believes mistakes destroy relationships needs repeated experiences of forgiveness and accountability existing together.

The operating system changes when reality repeatedly challenges its old predictions.

Accountability Builds Safety

Accountability is often misunderstood.

It is not humiliation.

It is not punishment.

It is not endless guilt.

Accountability is the willingness to own the impact of your behaviour without defending it.

To apologise without conditions.

To repair where possible.

To accept consequences.

To practise different choices.

To remain committed when change becomes uncomfortable.

Accountability is one of the strongest builders of emotional safety.

Repair Is More Powerful Than Perfection

Healthy families are not conflict free.

Healthy families repair.

Parents apologise.

Partners listen.

Children are heard.

Boundaries are respected.

Trust is rebuilt.

Repair teaches something profound.

Relationships can survive mistakes when people take responsibility for them.

Children who experience repair learn hope.

Adults who experience repair learn trust.

Human systems become stronger through consistent repair.

Building a Different Legacy

Many people spend years asking,

"Why did this happen to me?"

Eventually another question becomes more important.

"What will happen because of me?"

Every day we teach the people around us something about relationships.

About conflict.

About love.

About power.

About safety.

About accountability.

The legacy we leave is not written at the end of our lives.

It is written in the ordinary moments people experience with us every day.

The Human System You Leave Behind

Imagine your children describing home twenty years from now.

What do you hope they remember?

Not your income.

Not your achievements.

Not the size of your house.

How did home feel?

Could they speak honestly?

Were mistakes repaired?

Did they know they were loved?

Did they feel they belonged?

Did they believe they had worth simply because they existed?

That is the legacy of a regulated human system.

The Ripple Can Change

The greatest lie survival tells us is,

"This is just who I am."

It is not.

It is who your operating system learned to become.

Human systems continue learning for as long as we continue living.

The ripple is not permanent.

It changes every time someone chooses awareness over denial.

Responsibility over blame.

Repair over pride.

Connection over control.

Safety over fear.

That is how generations change.

Not through one perfect decision.

Through thousands of intentional ones.

Reflection

Take a moment to think about your own operating system.

What has it protected?

What has it cost?

What strengths has it given you?

What patterns no longer belong in the future you want to build?

Now ask yourself one final question.

If someone learns how to love, lead and live by watching me...

What will they learn?

Every human system is teaching the next human system.

The question is never whether we are leaving a legacy.

The question is whether we are leaving one built upon fear or one built upon safety.

The ripple changes the moment one person chooses to build a different human system than the one they inherited.

Chapter 13

Building Homes Where Safety Stays

"Safety is not created by accident. It is created through repeated choices."

Safe homes are not built because people never disagree.

They are built because people repeatedly choose behaviours that strengthen trust instead of fear.

Every home teaches something.

Every conversation teaches something.

Every repair teaches something.

Every boundary teaches something.

Every apology teaches something.

The question is never whether your home is teaching.

The question is what it is teaching.

Safety Is Built Every Day

Many people imagine safety as one decision.

It is not.

Safety is created through thousands of ordinary moments.

How we greet each other.

How we respond to mistakes.

How we manage conflict.

How we speak under pressure.

How we repair after hurting someone.

How we respect boundaries.

How we handle disappointment.

Human systems become safe because safe behaviours become normal.

The Five Foundations of a Safe Human System

Every emotionally safe home shares common foundations.

1. Emotional Safety

People can express thoughts and feelings without fear of humiliation, intimidation or punishment.

Disagreement is allowed.

Emotion is welcomed.

Repair is expected.

2. Physical Safety

No one fears being harmed.

Threatened.

Restrained.

Intimidated.

Or controlled.

Safety is never conditional.

3. Psychological Safety

People are allowed to think differently.

Ask questions.

Admit mistakes.

Learn.

Grow.

Without fear of rejection.

4. Relational Safety

Love is not earned through performance.

Respect is mutual.

Boundaries are honoured.

Trust is built through consistency.

5. Accountability

Everyone makes mistakes.

Everyone owns them.

No one is above repair.

No one is above responsibility.

Accountability protects relationships.

Not perfection.

What Children Need Most

Children need routines.

Predictability.

Warmth.

Boundaries.

Play.

Repair.

Curiosity.

Encouragement.

Most of all, they need adults who regulate themselves before attempting to regulate children.

Children learn emotional safety by experiencing it.

What Partners Need Most

Partners need respect.

Choice.

Honesty.

Freedom.

Support.

Repair.

Shared responsibility.

Healthy relationships are not built upon control.

They are built upon trust.

Trust cannot be demanded.

It is earned through repeated behaviour.

What Families Need Most

Families need conversations.

Not assumptions.

Curiosity.

Not criticism.

Leadership.

Not domination.

Consistency.

Not perfection.

The healthiest families are not the families with the fewest problems.

They are the families most willing to repair them.

Building Capacity Together

Healthy human systems build capacity together.

They encourage sleep.

Healthy routines.

Movement.

Connection.

Laughter.

Purpose.

Time together.

Time apart.

Rest.

Support.

They understand that every person brings different levels of capacity into each day.

Instead of asking,

"What is wrong with you?"

They ask,

"What has your day asked you to carry?"

That question often changes the conversation completely.

The Power of Repair

Every relationship experiences moments of rupture.

The difference is what follows.

Healthy human systems repair quickly.

They apologise.

Listen.

Understand impact.

Take responsibility.

Adjust behaviour.

Repair tells children something powerful.

Love is strong enough to survive mistakes.

Accountability makes relationships stronger.

Not weaker.

Safety Is Contagious

Fear spreads.

Control spreads.

Violence spreads.

So does safety.

So does kindness.

So does accountability.

So does respect.

Human systems constantly influence one another.

Every regulated adult increases the likelihood of another regulated interaction.

Every emotionally safe home strengthens the wider community.

The ripple works both ways.

Reflection

Think about your home.

If someone entered your home for one week, what would they learn about relationships?

Would they learn trust?

Respect?

Repair?

Accountability?

Or would they learn fear?

Control?

Silence?

Avoidance?

Every home is teaching.

What is yours teaching?

Homes do not become safe because conflict disappears.

Homes become safe because trust becomes stronger than fear.

Every ordinary interaction becomes another opportunity to teach the next generation what safety feels like.

Chapter 14

The Ripple We Leave Behind

"Every human system teaches the next human system what it believes about safety."

No human being lives in isolation.

Every conversation influences someone.

Every relationship teaches someone.

Every choice creates consequences beyond the moment in which it was made.

Whether we realise it or not, we are constantly shaping the human systems around us.

The question is not whether we create a ripple.

The question is what kind of ripple we leave behind.

Human Systems Create Human Systems

Children learn from families.

Families influence schools.

Schools influence communities.

Communities shape workplaces.

Workplaces influence leaders.

Leaders influence culture.

Culture influences families.

The ripple is continuous.

No human system exists on its own.

Every system becomes part of another.

That is why emotionally safe homes matter.

Their influence extends far beyond the walls that contain them.

Every Interaction Teaches Something

People are always learning from us.

Children.

Partners.

Friends.

Colleagues.

Neighbours.

Even strangers.

Every interaction teaches something about relationships.

How conflict is handled.

How mistakes are repaired.

How power is used.

How respect is demonstrated.

How emotions are expressed.

How accountability is practised.

The greatest lessons are rarely spoken.

They are lived.

The Ripple of Fear

Fear rarely stays where it begins.

It spreads.

Children who grow up expecting criticism often become adults who struggle to trust encouragement.

Adults who believe control creates safety may unintentionally build controlling workplaces.

Communities where fear becomes normal often stop asking difficult questions.

Fear narrows possibilities.

It reduces curiosity.

It limits connection.

The ripple quietly expands.

The Ripple of Safety

Safety spreads too.

One regulated parent teaches a child that mistakes do not threaten love.

One accountable leader teaches a team that honesty is valued.

One emotionally safe classroom teaches children that curiosity is welcome.

One respectful relationship teaches future generations what healthy love can look like.

The ripple works in both directions.

The question is where we choose to invest our influence.

Breaking the Invisible Inheritance

Many people inherit patterns they never chose.

Hypervigilance.

People pleasing.

Emotional shutdown.

Control.

Perfectionism.

Avoidance.

Shame.

These patterns are understandable.

They are not inevitable.

Every generation has an opportunity to decide what continues.

And what ends.

That decision rarely happens once.

It happens every day.

Building a Different Future

Imagine two children.

Both experience conflict.

One watches adults attack each other.

The other watches adults repair after disagreement.

Both learned something.

The question is what they learned.

Children are not simply learning what relationships are.

They are learning what relationships should be.

That lesson often becomes the blueprint they carry into adulthood.

The Courage to Change Direction

Changing a human system takes courage.

It requires noticing familiar patterns.

Questioning old beliefs.

Accepting responsibility.

Practising different choices.

Repairing when mistakes happen.

Continuing when change feels uncomfortable.

Healing is rarely dramatic.

It is usually ordinary.

Repeated.

Intentional.

The ripple changes through consistency.

Not perfection.

What Will Be Remembered?

Years from now, people may forget what you owned.

Where you worked.

How much money you earned.

They are far less likely to forget how you made them feel.

Did people feel safe with you?

Did children know they were loved?

Did your partner feel respected?

Did your colleagues feel heard?

Did your presence create calm or fear?

Legacy is rarely measured by achievements alone.

It is measured by the human systems we leave stronger than we found them.

The Wolfpack Way

The purpose of the Wolfpack Way has never been to create perfect people.

Perfect people do not exist.

The purpose is to build safer human systems.

Human systems where children grow up knowing they are loved.

Human systems where accountability is stronger than pride.

Human systems where repair is more common than blame.

Human systems where pressure is met with regulation instead of fear.

Human systems where the ripple becomes one of safety rather than survival.

That is how families change.

That is how communities change.

That is how generations change.

Reflection

Imagine someone describing you twenty years from now.

Not your career.

Not your achievements.

Your influence.

What would you hope they say?

What did your presence teach them about love?

About conflict?

About trust?

About safety?

About being human?

The answers to those questions become your legacy.

Every child becomes an adult.

Every adult becomes part of another human system.

Every human system teaches the next generation what safety feels like.

The ripple never stops.

The only question is whether it carries fear forward or whether it carries safety home.

Chapter 15

The Return Home

"The safest home a child will ever know begins with the adult who chooses to come home to themselves."

If you have reached this chapter, you have travelled a long way.

You have explored fear.

Pressure.

Capacity.

Identity.

Needs.

Control.

Violence.

Children.

Families.

The ripple.

Perhaps, for the first time, you have seen your own operating system more clearly.

Not to judge it.

But to understand it.

Understanding changes nothing by itself.

Choice does.

The Home We Carry

Many people spend their lives searching for home.

Some search through relationships.

Some through achievement.

Some through money.

Some through status.

Some through belonging.

Some through control.

Some through certainty.

Yet home was never meant to be only a place.

Home is also the human system we carry within us.

Wherever we go...

Our operating system goes with us.

Every relationship.

Every workplace.

Every friendship.

Every community.

We carry home into every room we enter.

The Child Within the Adult

Inside every adult lives a child who once asked three questions.

Am I loved?

Do I belong?

Do I have worth?

Some people received those answers consistently.

Many did not.

The child adapted.

The adult continued living.

Today, the questions may still appear.

Not because you are broken.

Because you are human.

Healing is not pretending those questions never existed.

Healing is finally answering them differently.

The Person You Needed

Many adults spend years wishing someone had protected them.

Listened to them.

Believed them.

Comforted them.

Encouraged them.

Loved them.

That grief is real.

Nothing in this book minimises it.

But eventually another question appears.

Can I become the person I once needed?

Not perfectly.

Not all at once.

One conversation.

One boundary.

One apology.

One act of courage at a time.

Every Choice Matters

Many people underestimate ordinary moments.

They believe change arrives through extraordinary events.

Usually it does not.

It arrives through ordinary choices.

Choosing to pause before reacting.

Choosing to apologise.

Choosing to listen.

Choosing to repair.

Choosing to seek help.

Choosing to rest.

Choosing honesty over avoidance.

Choosing accountability over blame.

Small choices repeated consistently become a different operating system.

The Ripple Begins With One Person

Every generation waits for someone to interrupt the pattern.

Someone willing to ask difficult questions.

Someone willing to accept responsibility.

Someone willing to choose differently.

That someone is rarely extraordinary.

They are simply the first person to refuse to continue what no longer serves the people they love.

History changes because ordinary people make extraordinary decisions repeatedly.

What Will Your Children Learn?

Whether you have children or not, someone is learning from your life.

A niece.

A nephew.

A student.

A colleague.

A friend.

A younger sibling.

A neighbour.

A future partner.

Every relationship teaches.

The question is simple.

When people experience you...

What do they learn about being human?

Coming Home

Perhaps home was never meant to be perfect.

Perhaps home was always meant to be the place where people know they are safe enough to become themselves.

That begins long before walls.

Long before furniture.

Long before addresses.

It begins with people.

People who regulate themselves.

People who repair.

People who tell the truth.

People who choose respect.

People who protect children.

People who understand that strength is measured by the safety they create around them.

That is what coming home truly means.

A Final Reflection

Close this book for a moment.

Think about the people who shaped your operating system.

Some helped.

Some hurt.

Some did both.

Now think about the people whose operating systems are being shaped by you.

What do you hope they remember?

Not your success.

Not your possessions.

Not your achievements.

How did they feel when they were with you?

Did they know they were safe?

Did they know they mattered?

Did they know they belonged?

Those memories become your legacy.

A Letter to the Reader

If no one has ever told you this before...

You were never meant to spend your life surviving.

You were never meant to believe fear was love.

You were never meant to carry responsibility for the choices other people made.

You were never meant to inherit pain without also inheriting hope.

Today, you understand something many people never stop to consider.

Human systems are learned.

That means they can also be rebuilt.

The past deserves to be understood.

It does not deserve to own your future.

You cannot change every chapter that came before today.

You can influence every chapter that comes after it.

You have that opportunity.

Every conversation.

Every apology.

Every boundary.

Every repair.

Every act of courage.

Every child who feels safe because of you.

Every partner who feels respected because of you.

Every human system that becomes stronger because you chose differently.

That is how the ripple changes.

Not through perfection.

Through people willing to become safe enough for others to grow beside them.

The future will never remember every word written in this book.

It will remember the homes that became safer because someone read it.

Thank you for choosing to become part of that ripple.

Welcome home.

The strongest human systems are not those that never experience pressure.

They are the ones that choose safety over fear, accountability over blame, and repair over repetition.

That is how homes change.

That is how generations change.

That is how the ripple finally comes home.

A Final Word

You have reached the end of this book.

But hopefully not the end of the conversation.

Understanding human systems is not about becoming perfect.

It is about becoming intentional.

Every relationship.

Every family.

Every community.

Every generation.

Begins with ordinary people making ordinary choices every day.

Some choices build fear.

Others build safety.

The future belongs to the choices we repeat.

If this book has helped you better understand yourself, your family, your work, or the people around you, then its purpose has already been fulfilled.

The Human Operating System is not about finding broken people.

It is about helping people understand that safer human systems create safer families, safer communities, and ultimately a safer world.

Thank you for becoming part of that ripple.

The Wolfpack Reflection Guide

Before You Close This Book

Take a moment to answer these questions honestly.

Safety

Do people feel emotionally safe around me?

How do I know?

Capacity

What currently builds my capacity?

What consistently drains it?

Identity

Who do I become when I feel under pressure?

Where did that version of me first develop?

Relationships

What patterns am I repeating?

Which ones deserve to continue?

Which ones deserve to end?

Ripple

What are the children in my life learning from me?

What are the adults in my life learning from me?

Legacy

If someone described my influence twenty years from now...

What would I hope they say?

The Wolfpack Family Safety Checklist

A healthy home is not perfect.

A healthy home is intentional.

Ask yourself:

☐ We apologise when we make mistakes.

☐ Children can express emotions safely.

☐ Adults regulate themselves before correcting others.

☐ Boundaries are respected.

☐ Conflict is repaired.

☐ People are not afraid to disagree.

☐ Love is not conditional.

☐ Accountability is expected.

☐ Respect is mutual.

☐ Home feels emotionally safe.

Every checked box strengthens the human system.

Every unchecked box becomes an opportunity to grow.

Continue the Journey

This book forms part of **The Wolfpack Way** collection.

Each book explores one part of the Human Operating System.

Start Here

The Triggered Wolf

Understanding why we react before we think.

Left Behind

How emotional abandonment shapes the adult operating system.

The Regulated Parent

Building homes children never have to recover from.

The Wolfpack Child

Helping children develop emotional safety and resilience.

The Regulated Teen

Understanding identity, adolescence and growing with purpose.

The Regulated Man

Strength that creates safety.

The Regulated Woman

Returning to yourself beneath survival.

The Regulated Leader

Building human systems where people thrive.

The Bullying System

Understanding behaviour under pressure across schools, workplaces and communities.

About the Author

Jyee Byrne is the founder of **Wolfpack Support Services** and the creator of **The Wolfpack Way**, an evidence-informed educational framework for understanding human behaviour through nervous system regulation, identity, capacity, relationships, and human systems.

His work was born from lived experience, years of supporting individuals and families, and a belief that behaviour makes far more sense when we understand the system beneath it.

Across schools, families, workplaces, community organisations, and leadership settings, Jyee's work focuses on one central idea:

Human systems create human systems.

Every conversation.

Every relationship.

Every environment.

Every generation.

The goal is simple.

Building Safer Humans.

For training, workshops, speaking engagements, books, and educational resources:

wpss.com.au

jyee@wpss.com.au

Discussion Guide

Individual Reflection

What part of this book challenged your thinking most?

Couples

How emotionally safe does our relationship feel?

What helps create that safety?

Parents

What emotional atmosphere does our home create?

What are our children learning from it?

Practitioners

Which parts of the Human Operating System could strengthen your current practice?

Organisations

How can understanding human systems improve the way your organisation supports families?

Acknowledgements

To every child who deserved greater safety.

To every adult courageous enough to examine their own operating system.

To every parent trying to create a different future.

To every practitioner, teacher, coach, leader and first responder working to protect families under extraordinary pressure.

And to everyone willing to believe that understanding and accountability belong together.

This work exists because of you.

Violence does not begin with violence.

It begins when human systems gradually lose the capacity to create and maintain safety.

The future changes when enough people choose to build homes where every child knows three things.

I am loved.

I belong.

I have worth.

The Wolfpack Way

Building Safer Humans

www.ingramcontent.com/pod-product-compliance
Lightning Source LLC
LaVergne TN
LVHW051923051126
851857LV00021B/2113
* 9 7 8 1 7 6 4 8 6 4 9 1 6 *